MOVING UP WITH SCIENCE

ELECTRICITY

PETER RILEY

PowerKiDS press

To my granddaughter, Holly Jane.

Published in 2017 by
The Rosen Publishing Group, Inc.
29 East 21st Street, New York, NY 10010

Cataloging-in-Publication Data
Names: Riley, Peter.
Title: Electricity / Peter Riley.
Description: New York : PowerKids Press, 2017. | Series: Moving up with science | Includes index.
Identifiers: ISBN 9781499431377 (pbk.) | ISBN 9781499431391 (library bound) | ISBN 9781499431384 (6 pack)
Subjects: LCSH: Electricity--Juvenile literature.| Electric power--Juvenile literature.
Classification: LCC QC527.2 R55 2017 | DDC 537--d23

Editor: Hayley Fairhead
Designer: Elaine Wilkinson

Photo acknowledgments: Baloncici/Shutterstock p4; Joe Belanger/Shutterstock p8b; Andy Crawford p19; Erika Cross/ Shutterstock p5; fotorince/Shutterstock p23b; Franklin Watts p12; KPY Ivary/Shutterstock p6b; Maksim Kazakov/Shutterstock p6t; Slawomir Kruz/ Shutterstock p15b; Marbury/Shutterstock p21b, p31t; Oleksy Mark/Shutterstock front cover inset; Ray Moller p8t, p9; Sergey Nivens/Shutterstock p7, p29; Somchai Rakin/Shutterstock p10b; weerayut ranmai/Shutterstock title page, p13, p28; RoadRunnerDeLuxe/ Shutterstock p21t; Seishin 90/Dreamstime front cover main; Dmitrij Skorobogatov/ Shutterstock p20t; STILLFX/Shutterstock p20b.

All other photographs by Leon Hargreaves.

With thanks to our models Sebastian Smith-Beatty, Layomi Obanubi and Crystal Kan.

Manufactured in the United States of America
CPSIA Compliance Information: Batch #BW17PK:
For Further Information contact Rosen Publishing, New York, New York at 1-800-237-9932.

All forms
of electricity
can be dangerous.
Always treat electrical
equipment with care.

Contents

Words in **bold** can be found in the glossary on pages 28–29.

How do we use electricity?

We use electricity every day. When we switch on a light or travel in a car, we are using electricity. Some pieces of electrical equipment are called **appliances**. Electrical appliances are machines powered by electricity, which help us in many different ways.

Electricity at home

Some electrical appliances give us heat so we can cook food or warm our homes. Some help move things, like spinning a disc in a DVD player or sending a toy car across the floor. Fridges keep food cold, lamps provide light, and radios produce sound. These are all common appliances.

Look at the items in this kitchen. How many electrical appliances can you see?

What electrical items can you see in this city?

Using electricity outside

Electrical equipment and appliances are not just found in homes. They power streetlights, traffic lights, pedestrian crossings and automatic doors on buildings. Even our vehicles' engines and lighting systems use electricity.

Make a list of the electrical equipment and appliances in your home. What is each item used for? Organize the list into groups according to what the appliances do: do they give heat or light, for example?

What is electricity?

Over two and a half thousand years ago in ancient Greece, a man called Thales did an experiment. He took a piece of **amber** and rubbed it, then put it near some straw and feathers. These objects jumped up to the amber and stuck to it. The Greek name for amber is "electron" and its strange power became known as electricity.

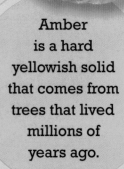

Amber is a hard yellowish solid that comes from trees that lived millions of years ago.

Static electricity

The electricity made by rubbing amber is called **static electricity**. Static electricity is a pulling force between two surfaces. You can **generate** static electricity by rubbing a dry wool cloth on a balloon. If you press the balloon to a wall, a pulling force between the two surfaces will hold the balloon in place.

Rub a balloon against a dry cloth and hold it above some pieces of tissue paper. Static electricity pulls the paper towards the balloon.

Storm clouds

The most powerful static electricity is generated in storm clouds. Inside the cloud, water **droplets** freeze and form ice crystals and hailstones. These rub together and generate static electricity.

Electric current

In a storm, huge amounts of static electricity are released as a **current** of electricity, which flashes through the air as lightning. We use much smaller currents of electricity in our electrical equipment and appliances.

Lightning can flash from cloud to cloud or, as pictured below, from a cloud to the ground.

You can charge a plastic pen with static electricity by rubbing it with a wool cloth. Test the pulling force by placing the pen near small, lightweight objects and describe any changes you see.

Cells and batteries

These batteries are boxes containing cells.

A **cell** is a store of electricity. A **battery** is a group of cells joined together. They are both used to make a current of electricity. Batteries can be used to power all sorts of things, including flashlights, laptop computers, mobile phones and some toys.

A cell is often shaped like a cylinder. These cells are also called batteries.

This car battery is made up of six cells joined together. They provide all the power for the car's engine, lights and electrical equipment, such as the radio.

Terminals of a battery

If you look closely at a battery, it has a plus sign (+) at one end and a minus sign (-) at the other end. The ends of a battery are called **terminals**. There is a positive terminal (+) and a negative terminal (-). To make electricity flow out of the battery, a **wire** must be in contact with each terminal.

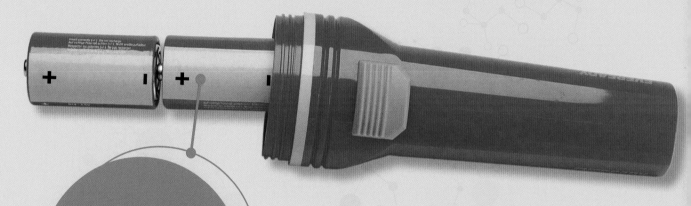

Two batteries are placed in a flashlight, with the positive terminal of one touching the negative terminal of the other.

Two batteries

Sometimes two batteries are joined together to generate more electricity. The positive terminal of one battery must touch the negative terminal of the other. If two positive terminals or two negative terminals are joined together, the electricity will not flow.

Find a toy that uses batteries and take them out (you may need an adult to help you). Look for the plus and minus signs on the batteries and on the inside of the toy. Can you put the batteries back in correctly and make the toy work?

A bulb

Bulbs are used to provide light. Some bulbs contain wires. When electricity passes through one of the wires, it gets so hot that it shines and gives out light.

Bulbs used in science

A bulb has two places where wires are attached. They are called **contacts**. The contacts are connected to wires inside the bulb. One of the wires inside the bulb is very thin. It is in the shape of a **coil**.

contacts

Bulbs used in experiments are very small and are screwed into plastic holders.

The light from inside these bulbs passes through the glass and lights up the street.

Lighting a bulb

You can make a bulb light up in the following way.

1. Attach one end of a wire to one terminal of the battery.

2. Attach the other end of the same wire to a contact of the bulb.

3. Attach one end of the second wire to the bulb's contact, and the other end to the battery.

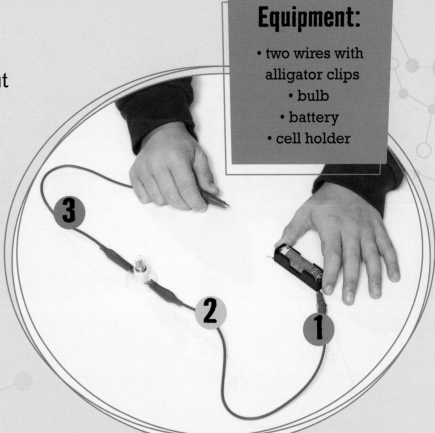

The flow of electricity

Electricity flows from the battery along a wire to the bulb. When it flows through the coil of wire in the bulb, the coil gets hot and glows. The electricity continues to flow out of the bulb, along the other wire and back to the battery.

The coiled wire in a bulb gives out light, which we can see through the transparent glass that surrounds the wire.

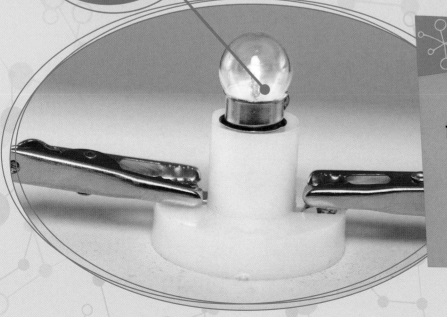

Describe the journey of an electric current flowing along a wire from a negative terminal, through the bulb and back to the battery.

Conductors and insulators

Wire is made of metal. Electricity can flow through it. A **material** which lets electricity flow through it is called an electrical **conductor**. Some materials do not let electricity flow through them. They are called **insulators**.

What happens to the bulb when you touch the wires to each different material?

Testing conductors and insulators

You can test materials to find out if they are conductors or insulators by setting up a battery and a bulb. Touch the ends of the wires to each material.

Conductors

If a material used in your experiment is a conductor, electricity will flow from the battery through the bulb, through the material, through the clips, and along the wire to the battery. When this happens, the bulb lights up to show that the electric current is flowing. All metals conduct electricity.

Insulators

If a material used in your experiment is an insulator, electricity cannot flow through it. It stops electricity flowing through the wires and bulb, and the bulb does not light up. Materials such as plastic, glass, paper, and wood are insulators.

AC electricity is generated by power stations. The electric current flows along metal wires to people's homes.

AC electricity is **EXTREMELY DANGEROUS** and can harm or even kill. You must treat all electrical equipment with care.

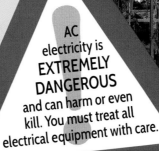

AC electricity

Alternating current (AC) electricity flows along conductors into plug sockets in your home. Insulators are used around the conductors to stop the current from harming you.

Why does a cable connecting a computer to AC electricity have a metal wire inside and a plastic cover on the outside?

A circuit

A **circuit** is the path that is set up for an electric current to flow. The parts of the circuit are called **components**.

Components of a circuit

The components of this circuit are a battery, a **switch** (see pages 18–19), a bulb, and the wires that connect them up. All the components in the circuit form a loop through which the current flows.

A switch controls the flow of the current in a circuit. If the switch is on, the current flows and the bulb lights up. If the switch is off, the current does not flow.

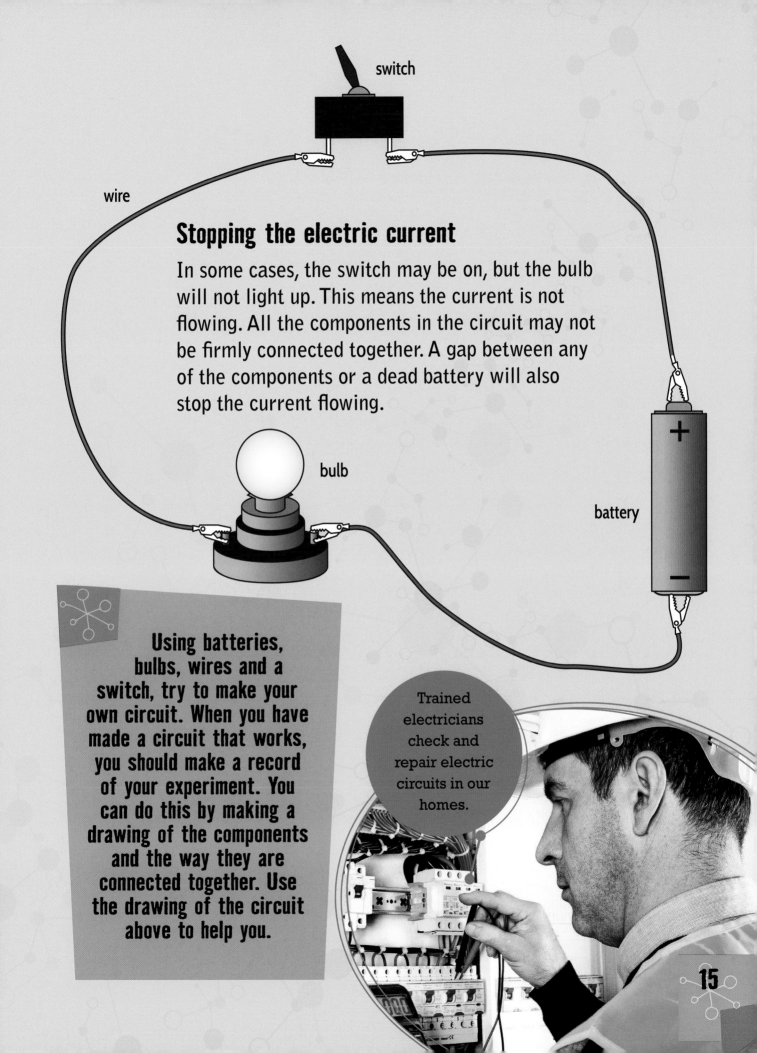

switch

wire

Stopping the electric current

In some cases, the switch may be on, but the bulb will not light up. This means the current is not flowing. All the components in the circuit may not be firmly connected together. A gap between any of the components or a dead battery will also stop the current flowing.

bulb

battery

Using batteries, bulbs, wires and a switch, try to make your own circuit. When you have made a circuit that works, you should make a record of your experiment. You can do this by making a drawing of the components and the way they are connected together. Use the drawing of the circuit above to help you.

Trained electricians check and repair electric circuits in our homes.

A series circuit

The correct way to make a circuit is to place all the components in a line in the circuit and join them together to make a loop. This type of circuit is called a **series circuit**.

Two bulbs in a series circuit

In the circuit below there are two bulbs. They are said to be arranged in series. When two bulbs are arranged in series they do not shine as brightly as just one bulb in a circuit, because the same amount of electric current is being shared between two bulbs.

Increasing the number of bulbs in a circuit makes them shine less brightly.

Increasing the number of batteries in a circuit makes the bulb shine more brightly.

Two batteries in a series circuit

In this circuit two batteries are arranged in series, so the negative terminal of one battery is connected by a wire to the positive terminal of the other battery. The two batteries give more power to the current and the single bulb shines more brightly.

What would happen to a bulb in a circuit if you added another battery in series? What would happen if you then added another bulb in series?

17

Switches

Switches are used to control the flow of electricity. When you need to use an electrical appliance, such as a computer or a light, you press or flip a switch and the electricity flows through it. When you have finished using the appliance, you press or flip it again and the current stops.

The switch is off, so the bulb does not light up.

Testing a switch

You can test a switch by attaching it to two wires that are connected to a battery and a bulb. When the switch is on, the electric current flows and the bulb lights up. When the switch is off, the electric current does not flow and the bulb does not light up.

Make your own simple switch

Loop your paper clip under one thumbtack. Push the thumbtacks into the wood so that the paper clip can touch both thumbtacks. Connect the wires to the thumbtacks using the alligator clips. The paper clip now acts as a switch and is ready to use.

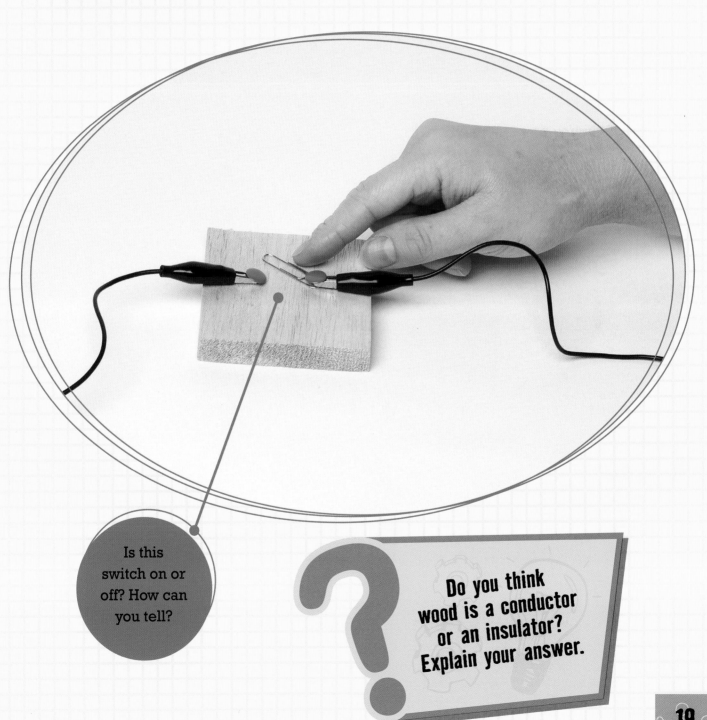

Is this switch on or off? How can you tell?

Do you think wood is a conductor or an insulator? Explain your answer.

19

Voltage

The power of a battery is called its **voltage** and is measured in units called **volts**. The symbol for this unit is V. You can see the voltage written on the side of the battery.

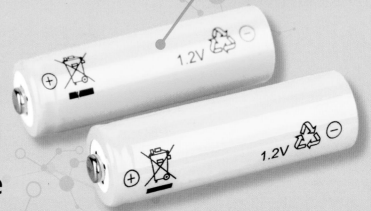

These batteries each have a voltage of 1.2V.

Increasing the voltage

When two batteries are joined together, the power of one battery is added to the power of the other. If two 1.5V batteries are joined together correctly in a circuit they give a power of 3V (1.5 + 1.5 = 3V). A battery can have a number of cells joined together inside it. This makes the battery more powerful than a single cell. Some batteries have a voltage of 4.5V, 6V or even 9V.

This 6V battery is used in large flashlights to provide a wide beam of light, or in a lantern where the bulb shines in all directions.

Voltage of a bulb

Bulbs are made to work at certain voltages such as up to 1.5V, up to 4.5V, and up to 6V. If a bulb is put in a circuit where the batteries supply a higher voltage than the bulb can take, then the coil of wire in the bulb gets so hot it melts and breaks, and the current stops flowing.

When the coil of wire in a bulb breaks, we say the bulb has burnt out.

If one Christmas light burns out, all the lights will go out if they are connected in series.

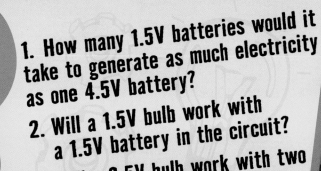

1. How many 1.5V batteries would it take to generate as much electricity as one 4.5V battery?

2. Will a 1.5V bulb work with a 1.5V battery in the circuit?

3. Will a 3.5V bulb work with two 1.5V bateries in the circuit?

Buzzers and motors

Buzzers and motors can be found in many electrical appliances. Buzzers can be used in burglar alarms. A buzzer makes a sound when electricity passes through it. Motors can be used in appliances such as fans. An electric motor has a **shaft**. Electricity passes through the electric motor, which spins the shaft.

The parts that produce the buzzing sound in a buzzer are delicate. They are protected by a plastic case.

A buzzer in a series circuit

A buzzer is designed to work up to a certain voltage. There is a label on the buzzer to show this voltage. A buzzer has a red wire and a black wire. It must be placed in the circuit carefully. The red wire must be attached to a wire coming from the positive terminal of the battery. The black wire must be attached to the wire coming from the negative terminal of the battery. If the wires are the wrong way around, the buzzer will not work.

battery

buzzer

A motor in a series circuit

A motor is also designed to work up to a certain voltage. There are two contacts on the motor where wires can be attached. The wires do not have to be attached in a special way, unlike the wires of the buzzer.

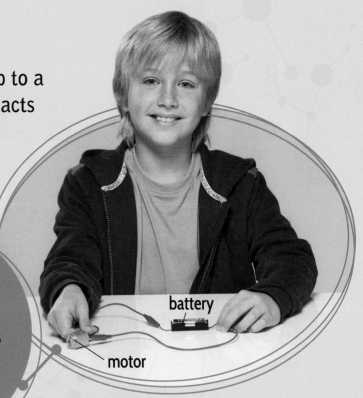

battery

motor

The motor shaft sticks out of a metal case. If you attach an object to it, the shaft will make the object spin around.

A motor spins this fan, which moves the surrounding air to produce a cooling breeze.

Look around your home for electrical appliances that turn things (but do not switch them on). Each one will have an electric motor. How many can you find? What does each appliance do?

A lighthouse

Electric circuits can be used to make models. You can make a model lighthouse, for example, using a simple circuit.

Equipment:

- plastic bottle
- bulb • three wires
- battery • switch
- small cardboard box
- **putty** • scissors
- adhesive tape
- thick card stock 1⅛ inch by 14 inch (3 cm by 35 cm)
- stopwatch

Building your lighthouse

1.
The main part of the lighthouse is made from a plastic bottle. Attach the bulb to the top of the bottle with some putty.

2.
Take the strip of card stock and bring the two ends together to make a circle. Stick the ends together with adhesive tape and place this over the top of the bottle so that it rests on top. Cut windows in each side of the small box and stick this to the circle of card stock to make your lantern room.

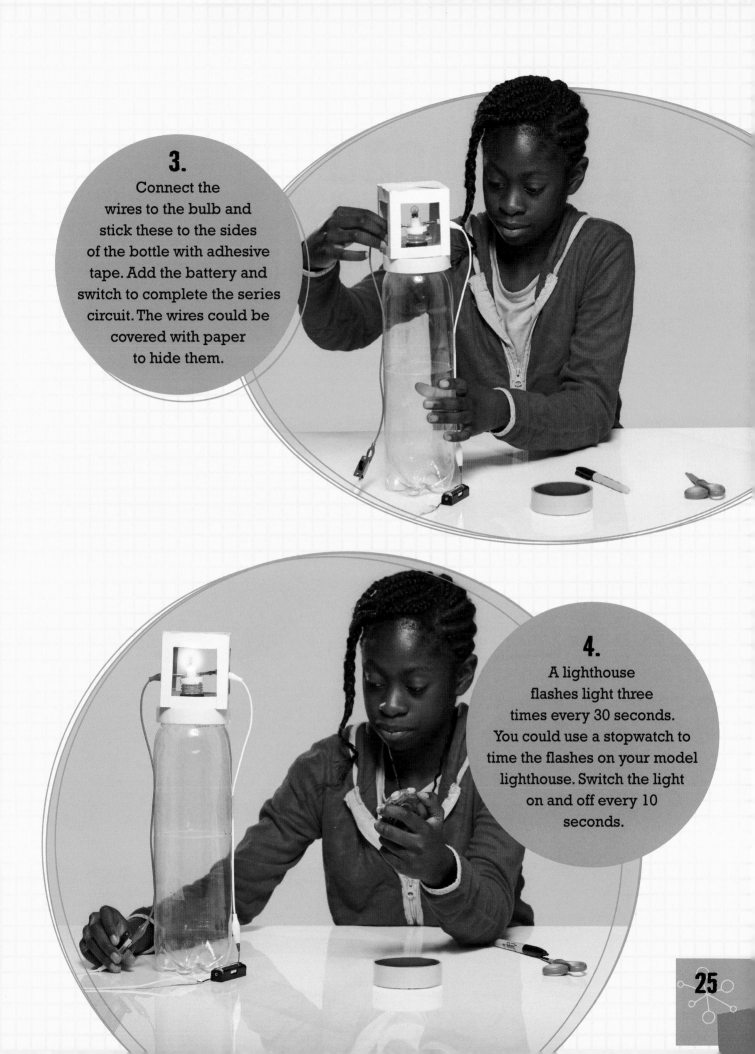

3.
Connect the wires to the bulb and stick these to the sides of the bottle with adhesive tape. Add the battery and switch to complete the series circuit. The wires could be covered with paper to hide them.

4.
A lighthouse flashes light three times every 30 seconds. You could use a stopwatch to time the flashes on your model lighthouse. Switch the light on and off every 10 seconds.

Robot head

You can make a robot head with two simple circuits. Make your robot's eyes light up – he can buzz too!

Equipment:

- large cardboard box
- scissors • adhesive tape
- two bulbs • switch
- two batteries
- small piece of cardboard
- aluminum foil
- wires • buzzer

1.
Create a circuit with the two bulbs, a switch and a battery. Cut two eye holes into the cardboard box and stick the bulbs inside them using adhesive tape. Cut a nose hole and stick the switch inside it. Cut a mouth hole and stick the battery inside it.

2.
When you tweak the robot's nose, you switch on the circuit and its eyes light up.

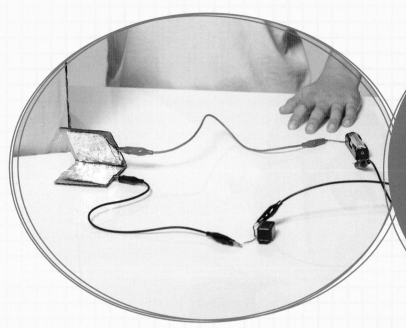

3.

To make your robot buzz when you pat his head, you will need another circuit and a homemade switch. Make the switch by folding a piece of cardboard and sticking two pieces of aluminum foil inside. Attach a wire to each piece of foil. Complete the circuit with a battery and a buzzer.

4.

Attach the switch to the top of the robot's head with adhesive tape. When you pat the robot's head, it buzzes!

What would happen if an extra battery was added to both of the circuits in the robot's head?

Glossary

Amber a honey-colored solid formed from the hardened juice made by trees that lived millions of years ago.

Appliance a machine powered by electricity that helps us, such as a washing machine.

Battery two or more cells joined together in a line. The positive terminal of one cell is connected to the negative terminal of the next. Cells are also usually called batteries.

Bulb a component in a circuit that gives out light when a current of electricity passes through it.

Cell a store of electricity. It contains substances that make a current flow round a circuit when the circuit is switched on. Cells are usually called batteries.

Circuit an arrangement of electrical components looped together so that when they are all connected, electricity flows.

Coil a length of wire that has been curled around into a row of circular loops.

Components the pieces of equipment that make up parts of a circuit, such as wires, bulbs, and batteries.

Conductor a material that allows a current of electricity to pass through it. Metal is a conductor.

Contact a place on an electrical component where a wire is attached to make part of a circuit.

Current the flow of electricity.

Droplet a very tiny drop.

Generate to make electricity, such as by rubbing a balloon on wool. Substances in a battery generate electricity when a circuit is switched on.

Insulator a material that does not allow a current of electricity to pass through it. Plastic is an insulator.

Material anything that contains matter in one of its three states: solid, liquid, or gas.

Putty a sticky substance used to join items together.

Series circuit a circuit in which all the components form a line.

Shaft the section or part spun around by a motor.

Static electricity a form of electricity made by rubbing two things together. Static electricity does not flow or move like an electric current.

Switch a component that controls the flow of electric current in a circuit by letting it flow or stopping it.

Terminal the part of a battery that is attached to a wire in a circuit. Electricity flows from the negative terminal to the positive terminal.

Volt a unit that measures the power of electricity.

Voltage a measure of the power of a battery in volts.

Wire a long, thin strand of metal that conducts electricity. Wires are usually covered in plastic.

Answers to the activities and questions

Page 5 How do we use electricity?

Activity: This will vary with each home. Examples are a kettle, iron or hairdryer to provide heat; lamps to provide light; a motor in a food processor to mash up food.

Page 7 What is electricity?

Activity: You should rub a plastic pen with a dry wool cloth about ten or more times and bring it very close (without touching) to some torn-up pieces of paper. The tiny pieces of paper will jump towards the pen.

Page 9 Cells and batteries

Activity: The toy should work when it is switched on. This shows that the batteries are arranged correctly and have a store of electricity. The batteries are usually held in with springs to make sure they make firm contact with the wires in the circuit.

Page 11 A bulb

Activity: An electric current flows from the negative terminal along the wire to the bulb. As the current flows through the bulb, it heats up the coil and makes it shine and give out light. The current then flows along the next wire to the positive terminal of the battery.

Page 13 Conductors and insulators

Answer: The metal wire is a conductor of electricity and lets the electric current flow to the computer. The plastic in the coating is an insulator and stops the current of electricity from leaving the sides of the wire.

Page 15 A circuit

Activity: Here are some examples of circuits you could draw:

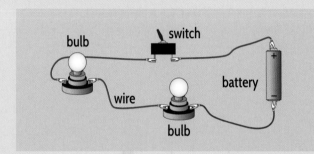

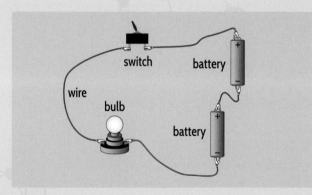

Page 17 A series circuit

Answer: It would get brighter. The bulbs would get dimmer.

Page 19 Switches

Answer: The switch is off because the paper clip is not touching the other thumbtack. Wood is an insulator. If it was a conductor, the current of the electricity would pass from one thumbtack to the other when the switch was off and the current would flow all the time.

Page 21 Voltage

Answers: 1. Three 2. Yes 3. Yes

Page 23 Buzzers and motors

Activity: Motors can be found in microwaves to make the turntable spin or in DVD players to make a DVD spin.

Page 27 Robot head

Activity: Be careful to keep the two circuits separate in the model. If two batteries are added to each circuit, the eyes shine more brightly and the robot buzzes more loudly.

Index